Sports Edition:

The Athlete

Tips To Maximize Your Potential

D. Best

3G Publishing, Inc.
Loganville, GA 30052
www.3gpublishinginc.com
Order No.: 888-442-9637

First published by 3G Publishing, Inc., September, 2013

ISBN: 978-0-9854968-7-6

eISBN: 978-0-9854968-9-0

Printed in the United States of America

Contents

Preface

If you would have asked me ten years ago, no five years ago about writing KWIK Tips for youth sports, I would have said, "Are you kidding me"! However, having a son who has been in youth sports since he was a toddler and the experiences we have encountered inspired me to share what we know.

Being a part of youth athletics since childhood and being around individuals who have come through the ranks and made it to the professional level as athletes and coaches gives me a different perspective on what to expect and what should be done. The experiences we gained over the years have been invaluable. There have been good experiences and bad experiences, good coaches, bad coaches, good team parents, bad team parents, winning teams and losing teams. And believe it or not there is something to learn from every experience. There are no regrets. Our team of experts has taken every experience and developed KWIK (Know What I Know) tips for you.

Remember, athletes need to play hard and have fun while doing it!

Introduction

If you are reading this book, you have made the first step in trying to better yourself as an athlete. This book is specifically written for youth athletes to provide them with quick tips in maximizing their potential.

Many youth sit back and dream of playing for their favorite college team and/or professionally one day. They picture themselves running for the winning touchdown, catching an unbelievable pass, hitting a home run or making the winning basket in the last second of the game. A lot of hard work, perseverance and skills increase the chances of this dream becoming a reality for youth athletes.

There are millions of youth who play sports. However, only a few will be offered college scholarships and fewer will become professional athletes. Some youth thinks it just happens by osmosis. They figure it is their dream; it is what they want to do; so, it will happen. However, some youth athletes actually understand the concept of a process and want to know how they can make it to the next level and the steps they need to take to get there.

Today, with the rise of competitive youth sports, the competition is great. So, youth athletes must do even more at an earlier age to standout and make people take notice of them. They cannot be the average athlete and do what everyone else is doing. Youth athletes who want to make it to the next level must go above and beyond. That will require discipline, focus, structure, diligence and determination.

The average person may not understand the magnitude of responsibilities placed upon student athletes, especially those striving for the next level. It is not as easy as it seems. A lot is expected of student athletes and they have very little free time in their day. But, the reward at the end is worth it especially, if they get a college scholarship and possibly continue to do what they love to do professionally.

Below are tips to assist youth athletes in reaching their highest potential. To be honest, it will not be an easy journey. There will be sacrifices. There will be bumps in the road. There will be times when you want to quit. That is the reality. However, understand that some of the greatest athletes of their time had some of the same obstacles. But, they never gave up. Hopefully this journey will be one that you will enjoy, learn a lot of valuable life lessons and have fun while doing it.

Statistics
Goals
Passion
Commitment/Responsibility
Practice: Team, Individual & Specialty Training
The Event
Equipment
Confidence
Attitude
Balancing Academics, Athletics & Rest
Leader/Role Model

Chapter I

Statistics

Many youth athletes have an unrealistic expectation on the number of athletes who obtain college scholarships and the number who move on to become professional athletes. Below are some statistics from the National Collegiate Athletic Association (NCAA) that will hopefully provide a more realistic picture.

Estimated Probability of Competing in Athletics
Beyond the High School Interscholastic Level

Student Athletes	Men's Basketball	Women's Basketball	Football	Baseball	Men's Ice Hockey	Men's Soccer
High School Student Athletes	535,289	435,885	1,095,993	474,219	35,732	411,757
High School Senior Student Athletes	152,940	124,539	313,141	135,491	10,209	117,645
NCAA Student Athletes	17,890	16,134	69,643	31,999	3,891	22,987
NCAA Freshman Roster Positions	5,111	4,610	19,898	9,143	1,112	6,568
NCAA Senior Student Athletes	3,976	3,585	15,476	7,111	865	5,108
NCAA Student Athletes Drafted	51	31	253	693	10	37
Percent High School to NCAA	**3.3%**	**3.7%**	**6.4%**	**6.7%**	**10.9%**	**5.6%**
Percent NCAA to Professional	**1.3%**	**0.9%**	**1.6%**	**9.7%**	**1.2%**	**0.7%**
Percent High School to Professional	**0.03%**	**0.02%**	**0.08%**	**0.51%**	**0.10%**	**0.03%**

Note: These percentages are based on estimated data and should be considered approximations of the actual percentages.

Last Updated: September 17, 2012

The statistical information was obtained from:
NCAA Research (2012, September). Probability of Competing In Athletics Beyond High School. Retrieved June, 2013 from http://www.ncaa.org/wps/wcm/connect/public/NCAA/Resources/Research/Probability+of+Going+Pro

Chapter 2

Goals

Before you set out on a journey, it is best to know where you are, where you are going and how you are going to get there. Having a plan will save you a lot of time, money and energy. If you are an athlete who aspires to go to the next level, you must plan your progress. After reviewing the NCAA statistics, hopefully, that will assist you in setting realistic goals and expectations.

First, ask yourself a few questions. Why are you participating in the sport? What do you want out of it? Is it for a college scholarship? Is it to become a professional athlete one day? Or, is it just something for you to do? Once you have identified your purpose that will help you set your goals. Of course, if your goal is to compete at a collegiate level or professionally, you will need to set long-term goals in addition to short-term goals. Short-term goals are measurable targets you want to accomplish in the near future. Long-term goals are measurable targets you want to accomplish over time. It is best to write your goals down so that you can review and track your progress over time. By doing so, you can see what you may need to focus on more or change.

Goal Setting Example 1:

If you currently run a 9-minute mile, your short-term goal may be to run an 8½ -minute mile within two weeks. Your long-term goal may be to run a 7-minute mile in 2 months. But, you must have a plan in order to get there. What do you have to do to increase your speed and shorten your time? It is a combination of several things, running consistently several times per week; leg strengthening exercises; stretching; racing others or running with a partner; increasing your stride rate, and timing yourself to see progress are just to name a few things. Keeping track of your runs by documenting your times will assist you in measuring your progress.

Goal Setting Example 2:

If your short-term goal is to increase your free throw shooting percentage from 20% (2 shots out of 10) to an average of 40% (4 shots out of 10), then you need to practice shooting shots from the foul line daily or as often as possible. It should be a consistent routine outside of regular practice. Free throw practice should focus on technique and you should have a set number you plan to shoot each time so that you can measure your success. For example, you may shoot 2 or 3 sets of free throw shots and focus on technique and routine. Repeating the same techniques or repetition will create muscle memory. This builds confidence during game time situations, because your shot should be automatic. Your long-term goal may be to increase it to 75% or greater.

The above examples should help you understand how to set goals. They must be measurable so that you can track your progress. Depending upon your sport will determine your goals and the steps you will need to take in order to reach them. Your long-term goal may be to get an athletic scholarship to pay for a college degree. However, you need to write down the steps you are taking in order to better yourself and stand out among the rest of the athletes now?

As you can see based on the NCAA statistics, a very small percentage of high school athletes get college scholarships. The number is even smaller for those college athletes who become professional athletes. The competition is great and it is not easy. Only the strong will survive. So make sure you have a plan. That plan may change over the course of time and that is all right because as you develop and mature opportunities may change. However, the key point here is to have a plan.

Most successful professional athletes did not become a star or master their craft overnight. It was a process. So do not think that you can wake up one day, work out for 3 months and be a star athlete at your school. Or, start working out for basketball tryouts a week or two prior. Most likely you will not make the team. Those who have a plan, practice and play consistently will most likely be the ones who progress to the next level.

Chapter 3

Passion

Some people participate in a sport because they want something to do. Some participate because they have a passion for it. Those individuals live it everyday. It is a part of their life. They study, practice and execute their craft. Having a passion for your sport separates the serious athletes from the average athletes.

Passion is what drives a person to want to do more. As with anything, your desire to participate in a sport will determine your level of commitment and affect your attitude. If it is something you want to do and you are passionate about it, you will have no complaints going the extra mile. You will give it your all no matter what.

However, there will be times when youth athletes are encouraged to participate in more than one sport and that second sport is not one that they desire to participate in. It can be a struggle. But, athletes need to look at the positive side of things. Each sport builds and enhances different skill sets and muscle groups. Those enhancements will ultimately make the athlete better and inevitably better in their sport of choice. For example, an athlete may love basketball, but have a lesser desire for track and field. However, track and field can build an athlete's endurance to run up and down the court during a basketball game or sprint to the other end of the court with ease. Playing football can assist with building strength and aggression that the youth athlete may not necessarily get with playing basketball alone.

Our advice is for the athlete to give 100% regardless. Look at the good in everything. Consider participating in the second sport of choice as a method of enhancing your skills and abilities. When it is time to participate in the first sport of choice again, you will enter the game or event with an even better athletic ability.

Chapter 4

Commitment/Responsibility

Commitment and responsibility separates serious athletes from those who just want to be a part of a team to wear a jersey or uniform. As an athlete, you must make the commitment to be a part of the team and accept the responsibility that comes with it. In order to reach the next level, athletes must be committed to themselves, their coaches and their teammates. If you are on a team, they depend on you regardless of your role or position, how long you play in a game or if you are a starter or not. If you are on the team, you are needed. Therefore, you must be there mentally and physically to support the team.

Commitment to the coach consists of the athlete arriving to practice, an event or game when scheduled and on time. If you are early, you are on time. If you are on time, you are late. If a coach says practice begins at 6 p.m., it begins at 6 p.m. Meaning, the athlete is ready to practice beginning at 6 p.m. not the athlete arriving at 6 p.m. and then taking 10 minutes to get ready for practice. If you are committed to the coach you should respect that individual as an authority figure and listen to what he or she has to say. The coach is present to help you improve as an athlete and to teach the team how to win. The information they provide during a game, event or during practice are strategies to help better you as an athlete and the team as a whole. Athletes must listen and pay attention at all times so that they are ready to execute what is being said.

Commitment also means no horse playing during practice. But, paying attention to instructions and what is being taught. As an athlete, one must be accountable and responsible for his or her actions. There is a time and place for everything. Horse playing, talking to your friends about the day's events and what you plan to do over the weekend is not appropriate during practice time. Athletes need to focus on what is taking place so that they can learn their part to help the team win.

Athletes, who are committed, persevere, work hard and pay attention. They put their best effort forward. That commitment will eventually pay off and the athlete will see the fruits of his/her labor. Athletes will get better as time progresses and they will see improvement in their skills and abilities. If athletes are doing what they are supposed to do, they should see improvement in their performance when comparing how they were at the beginning of the sport's season to the end of the season. If an Athlete does not see progression, something is wrong. It is usually one of two things, the athlete or the coach. Evaluate the situation and see who or what needs to change.

Chapter 5

Practice: Team, Individual & Specialty Training

Practice, practice, practice! You will hear that over and over again. You can never practice too much. Remember the saying "Practice makes perfect." This is a little stretch because no one is perfect. But, practices well help you maximize your potential.

Practicing for a sport consists of a variety of methods. Depending upon the sport will determine your workout routine. Most team practices will focus on techniques, routines, patterns, game plays, etc. However, your individual and specialty practices are where you maximize your ability as an individual to perform. The more you practice something it becomes like second nature to you. You do it without necessarily thinking. That is why it is always important for you to practice like you are going to play or perform because you are creating a habit or muscle memory.

Athletes need to make the most out of their practice time. Practices are not play dates. They need to take practices seriously. Athletes need to be present both physically and mentally. They should arrive to practice early enough to change into their practice gear, warm-up and prepare to work hard or go home. Loafing, playing around, talking, and not hustling and any of the like are not acceptable behaviors during practice time. There is a time and place for socializing and practice time is not it. Athletes need to stay alert and cooperate so they can focus on reaching their personal best. Remember, how you practice is most likely how you are going to perform when it counts. Coaches know that and usually use practice time to determine game playing time. So, take the initiative, do what you have to do and make the most out of your practice time.

The team's practice time is exactly what it means - team. It is not individualized for each athlete. The coach may tell you what you need to work on during your own time, but the team's practice will focus on how your role integrates with the team.

The coach will instruct athletes on their role or position within the team as he orchestrates each move. Athletes need to focus on what is being taught, replicate it several times so that they can prepare to execute what is being taught during the game or event.

The average athlete will go to regular practice, do what is required of the team and may practice a few things at home. Years ago that type of routine was acceptable and athletes excelled. However, due to today's competitive level, that type of workout routine will not work for those striving to reach the next level. Athletes today who are striving for the next level must do things above and beyond the average athlete. If they want to compete at the next level, they need to practice with their team, individually and have specialty training.

Specialty trainers typically specialize in certain positions and techniques for different sports. Just to name a few, there are hitting and pitching coaches for baseball, quarterback and receiver coaches for football, speed coaches for sprinters, and ball handling and shooting coaches for basketball. These specialized trainers will help the athlete learn new techniques and improve their current skill set that will allow them to have an advantage over others. It is common to see these types of trainers working with college and professional athletes. However, we are increasingly seeing more youth athletes take advantage of these specialty trainers as well.

Athletes should always have athletic homework after each practice. The completion of this homework will inevitably improve their skills as an athlete. There is always something an athlete can work on individually at home. They may have to practice a routine, learn a game play, shoot free throws, or practice a move or technique. Whatever, it may be, it will be up to the individual athlete to make sure that it happens.

Remember your team is counting on you to know your part. You will have to study and practice. That is how you will escalate your game IQ and your performance. Preparing for game days is similar to preparing for a test you may have for class. The more you study and understand what is being taught, the more likely you are to ace the test. The same holds true with a competition. The more you prepare by practicing, developing your sports IQ and doing things on your own the more prepared you are to reaching your personal best.

"I play to win, whether during practice or a real game. And I will not let anything get in the way of me and my competitive enthusiasm to win."

Michael Jordan

Practice like you are going to play!

Chapter 6

Equipment

Athletics are becoming more physically aggressive and although protective gear will not totally prevent injuries, it will limit the number and maybe severity of injuries. Therefore, it is very important that athletes protect themselves from head to toe. Depending upon the sport, there is different protective gear required and recommended for each sport. Protective gear can range from but not limited to helmets, goggles, elbow protectors, mouthpieces, padded undergarments, gloves, kneepads, shin pads, ankle protectors and shoes.

Furthermore, athletes need to understand that equipment can be very expensive and costly to those who have to purchase it. Athletes need to be responsible individuals and keep up with and take care of their equipment.

Chapter 7

The Event

It's show time! No matter the sport, all athletes anticipate the day they get to compete. It is on this day that athletes get to see the results of all of their hard work and sweat equity. This is the time they bring everything together; what they learned in practice, on their own and with their specialty trainer. Although this day brings uncountable emotions for all who participate, the one thing the athlete needs to remember is to have fun regardless of what happens.

The day of competition whether it is a game or another type of sporting event requires mass preparation from all who are in involved in making the event happen. The main attraction or star on that day is the athlete. People come to watch them or their team compete as a form of entertainment. The athlete's role is critical, because their attitude, effort, and abilities can positively or negatively impact and influence the outcome of the game or event.

It is critical for athletes to understand what is expected of them and the different situations that may arise during the game or event. The type of event will definitely yield different situations, however, there are several experiences that crossover no matter the type sport.

Showcase

Not only are you doing what you love to do but you are also showcasing your talent. People love a good show. They enjoy seeing a good competition. Your job as an athlete is to go out there and do what you do best. Compete and have fun. You never know who is at a sporting event watching, so you should always perform to the best of your ability. At times there are college as well as professional team scouts, coaches and players among the spectators. They could be in the crowd for business purposes looking for new talent or there to support a relative or friend. Needless to say, for whatever reason they are there they will notice those individuals who stand out. So, perform to your best ability.

Playing Time

This is a sensitive topic and generally is the root of all evils in disagreements between parents and coaches. However, once you reach a certain age in a competitive sport, the athlete determines his or her playing time. The coach's goal is to win. The athlete's goal is to play to the best of his or her abilities. The athlete's practice time should determine his/her playing time. If an athlete is serious, discipline, listens, has a good attitude and works hard during practice, they will exhibit the same type of behavior during game time situations. The coaches recognize this and will reward those individuals with playing time.

If a game is very close from the aspect of winning or losing, a coach will most likely only play the best players. This is generally because the coach can trust the athletic abilities and skills of those individuals to assist in winning the game. Taking the risk of playing an individual who skills are not up to par could cause the team to lose in a close game situation and depending upon the situation put the coach's job in jeopardy. I know as an athlete all you want to do is play. However, there is a bigger picture here. Several things are at stake. Just do what you need to do in practice and during the game and the coach should not be able to deny you playing time.

Team

So often people would say if it was not for this person or that person the team would not have won. Or, that person was the only one who played. REALLY? If it is a team sport, it takes the whole team to win. Otherwise, just put that one player out there by himself or herself and see what happens. TEAM stands for Together Everyone Achieves More. Now, one or two individuals may stand out from the other players and bring a little more to the team, but all contribute to the game or event. In a team sport, you must be willing to work with others and not individually. It is very obvious when teams play individually and not as a team. Games have been lost due to selfish thinking. Remember, teams achieve more if everyone works together.

Additionally, everyone needs to feel like they are contributing to the game. It is very apparent which athletes and teams understand the meaning of teamwork and have a team concept. Athletes who understand the true meaning of TEAM work very well together and have chemistry. They understand that it takes more than one or two players to win and ensures everyone is involved. Everyone has a role on the team and everyone can contribute otherwise they would not be there. So do not be a selfish player, but be a team player.

Each team member has a particular role on the team and can contribute a significant amount of their talent if they are allowed. Teammates need to support each other and provide words of encouragement. This promotes team spirit, increases team morale and boosts confidence levels among the team. If a teammate feels inclusive they are more than willing to give 100%.

External Distractions

An athlete's attitude can positively or negatively impact their performance. Several factors may contribute to this; their home situation, girlfriend or boyfriend, referees/officials, coaches, etc. However, when athletes come to play or perform, their focus need to be on that event, competition or game. They do not need additional unnecessary distractions. The competition should be their one and only focus. Athletes need to start mentally preparing themselves prior to arriving to the competition so that they are definitely focused when the time comes. That means no telephone conversations, texting, playing video games, etc. This takes discipline, but they do not need those types of distractions that may affect their performance.

At times during the game or event, athletes may get frustrated for several reasons. It could be because they are not satisfied with their performance, the referees may be making bad calls, their parents may be yelling from the stands or the coach is correcting an action. Whatever it is, they should not take it personally. Referees are not perfect and they will make bad calls at times. However, an athlete getting an attitude and pouting will not change the call or make the situation any better. They need to try to block out all distractions except for their coach's voice. Remember, the coach is on the athlete's side and wants them to do well. They see things that they may not see or realize, so they should listen and make any necessary adjustments.

Complacency

Athletes should never become complacent and feel as though they no longer need to work hard because they are in the starting line-up, getting a lot of playing time or winning the game. Remember there is always someone on the team waiting in line for that position and they are continuously working hard to achieve that goal. The losing team is steadily working hard to win. Athletes have to continue to work hard so that they can continuously get better, stay on top of their game and win the competition. Remember the event is not over until the buzzer sounds. Think about the story of the tortoise and the hare. The hare just knew he was going to win because he was faster than the tortoise. During the race, the hare became complacent, let his guard down and fell asleep. However, the tortoise continued to strive hard and won the race. Complacency will cause you to get beat if you are not careful. Even the best athletes continue to work hard. That is how they remain the best.

Over Confident

As stated earlier, the game is not over until the buzzer sounds. Do not get caught up in thinking that just because your team is ahead with a few minutes left in the game that your team has won. Time and time again, athletes have thought this and lost. Why? Most times it is because the team who is leading gets complacent and stops playing to the best of their abilities. But the other team is still playing to win. It has happened at all levels including college and professional. Please take this word of advice, no matter how much of a lead you have, continue to play hard.

Never Give Up

Never give up! This cannot be said enough. Always play to win and play until the end. There have been unbelievable comebacks because the athletes had heart. They wanted to win, kept their composure, worked hard and made it happen. Know that it can happen. Having heart or the will to win also ties into showcasing. Scouts and coaches observe how players react when they are losing. Yes, they want to see them win, but they also want to see how athletes respond when things are not going in their favor. An athlete's attitude and effort is just as important as his/her skills and abilities, because it defines that athlete as an individual.

Officials/Referees

Officials, Referees or Judges are at events to ensure the rules of the game or competition are being followed accordingly. As with athletes, these individuals are at various levels in their skills and abilities. However, bottom line, they are officiating the event and they rarely retract a call or decision that has been made. Knowing this, do not argue with the referees or talk to them if you are discontent. Understand that all decisions or calls are not going to be in your favor. Accept it and move on. Do not let them affect our game or performance.

Win or Lose

Athletes should always enter a competition with the mind-set of winning. Their thoughts should be those of a champion. No matter what the critics say and no matter what the predictions are, an athlete should always put their best foot forward. Remember, your attitude impacts your performance. If you think you are going to lose, most likely you will because, with that type of attitude, you have given up and are displaying defeat before you even compete.

Winners think like victors and display confidence in what they do. Athletes need to play to win instead of playing not to lose. There is a difference between the two phrases. If an athlete plays to win, they give 100% effort towards winning. They have a drive to compete and are motivated to win. Winning is their choice. Athletes who play not to lose are not exhibiting their full potential. They are present because of an obligation. Their performance is mediocre. They give just enough trying not to lose. Winners take risks. Individuals trying not to lose, play it safe.

Needless to say, we all know that there is a chance of losing even if an athlete has the attitude of winning. That is a reality. However, if an athlete worked hard, put forth their best effort and performed at the best of their ability, they are a winner whether they win or lose.

Chapter 8

Confidence

The one thing discussed among youth athletes and their parents is CONFIDENCE level. If athletes are not confident in what they are doing, it will affect their performance. There are several reasons an athlete's confidence level may be low. Sometimes it is because they are learning a new skill and they are not totally comfortable with their performance but most often it is because some adult, usually a coach, parent or spectator said or did something to the athlete that affected their level of confidence. Words are powerful and sometimes an untamed tongue cuts worse than a sharp knife.

As a youth, many look for validation from their coaches and other adults. Youth expect them to be their support system and to provide them with encouraging words, developmental opportunities and uplifting words of wisdom. An athlete's coach and other adults should be there for them and many are. However, there are a few adults who do not understand their role and impact on the development of a youth athlete and will strip the confidence of athletes for no other reason than to stroke their own ego or to show who is in charge. For some adults, it may be unintentional, but many know exactly what they are doing.

This is discussed in this book so that athletes can be prepared for reality. It is a part of life. Everyone that athletes or individuals encounter in life is not always going to be their friend or like them. Believe it or not, some want to see them fail. Many times it has nothing to do with what the athlete has done or has not done; it is because the other individuals are jealous for some reason or another and they want to bring the athlete down. Or, they are displacing anger on the athlete from another situation that may be going on. But, as an individual and athlete, one must have confidence in themselves that if they have done nothing wrong to keep their head up high and keep moving. Athletes need to be their number one fan and believe in themselves.

Additionally, there are some coaches who will yell, scream, call you out of your name; say you are nothing and that you are not going to be anything; say that you are not doing anything when you know you are; and uplift some athletes at the expense of criticizing others. Some coaches try to use these negative tactics to motivate youth athletes, others are just down right hateful. If this is happening to you and it is affecting you as an individual, you need to tell your parents. Some athletes may hear these things and it means nothing to them. It does not affect their performance in any way. However, there are quite a few athletes who take what is being said or done to them at heart and it really affects them mentally and negatively impacts their performance. Much has to do with their maturity level and age. Nonetheless, do not let anyone, a coach, official, parent or another athlete get into your head and negatively impact your performance.

A person's thoughts are powerful and impactful. How one views things will determine their perspective on life. If they think and say it is a good day, it will be a good day. If they think it is the worst day of their life and nothing is going right then most likely that is what is going to happen. Individuals determine their happiness. They should not depend on others to make them happy.

Youth athletes must realize that we all make mistakes. No one is perfect. While watching many youth sports games, several coaches and adults forget about that and expect their child and other youth athletes to be perfect. In basketball, adults have told a child not to shoot because he missed a shot earlier. However, professional athletes strike out in baseball, miss passes in football, and miss jumpers and basic lay-ups in basketball. As noted above, the action words used are plural, meaning it has happened several times in many professional games. So, how can it be expected that the youth athlete will be perfect. From experience, professional athletes have learned not to give up. They do not stop. They go back and do it again and again until they get it right. Athletes must have the confidence that they will make the basket; hit the ball; and that they will catch the pass.

Athletes should also practice like they are going to play. They should work hard during their organized practices and work hard in their individual practices. Athletes build their confidence by maximizing their skills and abilities so that they can reach their highest potential. BELIEVE in yourself, THINK POSITIVE and good things will happen.

One of the greatest basketball players of all times said the following:

"I've missed more than 9000 shots in my career. I've lost almost 300 games. 26 times, I've been trusted to take the game winning shot and missed. I've failed over and over and over again in my life. And that is why I succeed." Michael Jordan

No one is perfect. Not even one of the greatest. Everyone makes mistakes, so, Never give up and Never stop trying.

Chapter 9

Attitude

Attitudes can be defined in several different ways. It can also define a person's character. Just like having confidence, an athlete's attitude is critical in his or her role as an athlete and individual. It can enhance or deflate his or her performance and career.

Take a look at professional athletes. We all know that not all professional athletes are popular and much has to do with their attitude and behavior on and off the court per say. If they are arrogant, disrespectful and disloyal to their fan base you will see very few endorsements from companies if any at all. Why? Companies give athletes endorsements to promote their products so that consumers or fans will buy the product. Companies want increased sales and to make money. If they do not feel the athlete can promote their product and help them make money, the company will not give the athlete an endorsement. Athletes who are likeable by many have more advantages than those who are not. The likeable ones have a fan base; get endorsements; typically have a longer career if they maintain their health; and other opportunities after retirement.

If athletes want to succeed and have the opportunity to do what they love to do everyday, they need to have the right attitude and mind-set. Those athletes who succeed work hard often and seldom complain. Athletes with the right attitude have very little excuses. They own up to their mistakes, try not to do it again and move on. Those who make excuses, complain, do not follow rules, shut down, pout and throw tantrums do not make it too far. Why? Coaches do not have time for that. They do not want to deal with a spoiled brat.

Additionally, some athletes may think that because they are talented or considered an elite player that the coach must and will tolerate their blasé and/or bad attitude because they need them on the team to win. They may also feel that they do not need to work hard. Some inexperienced coaches may find that acceptable. But, they are not helping that athlete's future. Veteran coaches who are good at what they do will not tolerate that type of behavior and will communicate their expectations. Athletes need to remember that there is always someone trying to get their spot on the team. Or, beat them in an event and that other athletes are working hard everyday. Coaches will invest their time in those athletes who show up for practice on time, go hard and consistently give 100%. Furthermore, your teammates will respect you and the fans will love you.

"Hard work beats talent when talent fails to work hard."

-Kevin Durant

At times, people confuse an athlete's confidence with arrogance and some people confuse arrogance with confidence. You can have confidence and not be arrogant. Humility is the defining factor. Pride and arrogance will cause you to miss out on many opportunities because most people will not advocate for you to move to the next level. Many professional athletes have missed out on additional opportunities because of their unsatisfactory behavior. The old folks had a saying. The same people you see going up are the same people you will see coming down. In other words, nothing is guaranteed. So, do not burn any bridges, remember where you came from and stay humble.

As a youth athlete, it is very important for you to remember that you need to have the right attitude. The way an individual behaves as an athlete and in life is critical. Youth athletes need to realize that their attitude can either promote or demote their athletic career. With the right attitude athletes can go far in life. People will go out of their way to help them reach their highest potential.

"True humility is not thinking less of yourself; it is thinking of yourself less."

C.S. Lewis

Chapter 10

Balancing Academics, Athletics and Rest

Student athletes must be disciplined, focused and diligent if they wish to succeed in both sports and academics. They must be able to balance school, homework, athletic workouts, practices, their social life and rest. Most adults find it difficult to balance everything and have a work-life balance. So, it is understandable that it may be difficult at first for a youth athlete to balance it all. However, once the athlete has a routine established, it should all fall into place. Student athletes must strive to have a sport-school-life balance. In addition, some may have the responsibility of a part-time job. All of these can be overwhelming and very demanding causing additional pressures and stressors to be placed upon them. Therefore, it is important for the student athlete to learn how to balance it all.

Most student athletes function very well with a structured schedule. A schedule keeps an individual on track and ensures nothing of importance is missed as long as it is followed. It is highly recommended that student athletes have a weekly schedule that includes their priorities first such as school time, workout time, practices and study time. This type of structure is nothing new. College athletes are typically on a strict schedule that incorporates workouts, practices, study hall, tutoring sessions, and class time. Those athletes must have a schedule to ensure they do not miss anything that is vital to them performing as a student athlete. Student athletes have to remember that academics and sports are interrelated. They must perform well in both if they wish to participate in school-sponsored athletics and graduate with a degree or diploma. For example, if a student athlete's grades are not meeting eligibility requirements, most times they will be suspended from participating in school sponsored athletics. Additionally, if the student athlete is not performing as expected in their given sport, they run the risk of several things happening. Their playing time may decrease. They may get cut from the team. Or, they may lose their scholarship for school. So, it is very important for the athlete to perform well in both.

All of this may sound demanding and it may not sound like a lot of fun. But, if it is a youth athlete's desire to go to the next level and succeed as a student athlete, he/she must be willing to make some sacrifices. Making sacrifices is difficult for anyone. However, most often for youth, it is what they may consider to be their "free" time. Most likely, the youth athlete will have to limit time fillers such as, watching television, playing video games, texting, talking on the phone, socializing with their friends, etc. Furthermore, some sports may require them to eat healthier and limit their intake of junk food, sugars, and fast foods. What youth athletes need to understand is that there is a time, place and season for everything. These things are not completely eliminated. They just have certain time restrictions depending upon the time of the year and the demands that may be placed upon the youth athlete at that time.

Lastly, it is very important for youth athletes to get the appropriate amount of rest so that they can keep up with the physical and mental demands that are placed upon them. A person's body needs time to recuperate and regenerate from the amount of physical activity it endures in a given day. The mind needs a chance to rest as well. People function better if they have the appropriate amount of rest. They are refreshed and have energy. This is hard for some youth athletes to comprehend, because they want to incorporate some of the time fillers into their rest time. But, they need to understand the importance of rest and how they need it in order to function better as an individual.

Chapter 11

Role Model/Leader

Whether athletes like it or not, people see them as role models and leaders. Their attitudes and behaviors have a great influence on others. So much that they want to be like them. Athletes are modern day gladiators providing entertainment to spectators who admire their skills and abilities as they perform amazing tasks set before them. Some of their talent is unforeseen, placing these individuals in an elite category above others.

Athletes are considered by many to be extraordinary. They cannot help but be in the spotlight. Therefore, their every move is critiqued, analyzed and evaluated. I know athletes do not ask for it. But, it comes with the territory. Accept that responsibility with humility and give back to those coming up behind you. Make a positive difference in someone else's life. Leave a legacy for others to follow. Do not let the increased attention, spotlight, and glamour change you, because you are amazing, just the way you are.

"Talent is God given. Be humble. Fame is man-given. Be grateful. Conceit is self-given. Be careful."

- John Wooden

Chapter 12

Conclusion

The message repeatedly throughout this book has been about perseverance, humility, setting goals, having the right attitude, possessing confidence and hard work. It is not expected that athletes will learn everything there is to know overnight. There is a learning process and the mind, body and soul will develop over time. Athletes will also blossom or peak in their own time. But, one must consciously and consistently work on what they need to improve. Some of the greatest athletes were cut from teams in high school, did not receive college athletic scholarships, and did not have the resources many youth have access to today. But, they never gave up. They continued to work hard and they still made it. Athletes can never work too hard and they should never stop learning. Athletes should continue to do things that will ultimately benefit them as an athlete, student and individual.

The reality is that many will start out on this journey but only a few will make it. Roadblocks, adversities or difficulties are often put in your paths, but it is up to you to figure out how you will handle it. Will you go around it, climb over it or allow it to stop you in your path? That decision will be yours to make. However, those who have a passion for what they love and believe in will not allow something to stop them from fulfilling their dreams. They will find a way to make it happen. They will not make excuses but come up with solutions. Focus on the things that you can control and make a difference in your life. Stay focused. Set goals. Know where you are coming from and know where you are going. You must have a plan. Believe in yourself, have faith, fear not and you will go far.

" Success is peace of mind which is a direct result of self-satisfaction in knowing you did your best to become the best you are capable of becoming."
- John Wooden

The quotes were obtained from:
Brainy Quote. Retrieved 2012 & 2013. http://www.brainyquote.com

www.ingramcontent.com/pod-product-compliance
Lightning Source LLC
Chambersburg PA
CBHW031334040426
42443CB00005B/339
9780985496876